MENTORING
ENGAGED AND
NEWLYWED
COUPLES

PARTICIPANT'S GUIDE

Building Marriages That Love for a Lifetime

DR. LES PARROTT III
& DR. LESLIE PARROTT

ZondervanPublishingHouse
Grand Rapids, Michigan

A Division of HarperCollinsPublishers

Mentoring Engaged and Newlywed Couples Participant's Guide
Copyright © 1997 by Les and Leslie Parrott

Requests for information should be addressed to:

ZondervanPublishingHouse
Grand Rapids, Michigan 49530

ISBN 0-310-21709-1

Interior design by Sue Vandenberg Koppenol

Printed in the United States of America

00 01 02 03 04 /❖ DH/ 10 9 8 7 6 5 4

*To the next generation of married couples
and those who walk beside them.*

CONTENTS

APPENDIX

An Important Message for Prewedding Mentors

Resources for Marriage Mentors

Marriage Mentor Meeting Report

Marriage Mentor Final Feedback Form

ACKNOWLEDGMENTS

In preparing this curriculum kit, many people were invaluable to us. On a rainy day in Seattle, over a leisurely lunch, Scott Bolinder caught the vision for creating a tool that could be used to build a national network of marriage mentors. His support is so consistent we fear taking it for granted.

Sandy VanderZicht and Rachel Boers at Zondervan provided exceptional editorial work on this project. Jeff Bowden's technological know-how and cinematic eye made the video piece of this curriculum practical and pleasing.

The expert advice of Norm Wright, who blazed the trail for marriage preparation many years ago, and Scott Stanley, whose empirical savvy on marriage burns like a beacon for those who take notice, served as guides to us in this process.

Mike McManus, the motivational giant of marriage mentoring, deserves special thanks for his yeoman work and our many coast-to-coast conversations that helped improve and refine this project.

Finally, we want to say thanks to the hundreds of couples in Seattle—both mentors and mentorees—who allowed us to bring them together in the Marriage Mentor Club. May your tribe increase.

INTRODUCTION

It was a lovely wedding, complete with professional-quality music. Everything went off without a hitch. Anne was gorgeous, Peter handsome. With such a picture perfect wedding, few gave thought to the inevitable turbulence that lay ahead for this new couple.

Very few considered the premarital counseling (or lack of it) Anne and Peter went through before the ceremony. And almost no one considered that, so soon after their honeymoon, Anne and Peter could benefit from a year-long process of meeting with a marriage mentor couple.

Quietly, however, more and more couples, counselors, and pastors are learning about the value of marriage mentoring—before and after the wedding. And since you are holding this Participant's Guide in your hand, it must have piqued your interest as well.

In fact, you are probably aware of this idea because a devoted pastor in your church recruited you. Marriage mentoring is a means by which ministers can fulfill Paul's injunction from the letter to the Ephesians where he says the job of a pastor is "to prepare God's people for works of service" (4:12). And we know of no other works of service that could be of more value in this age than marriage mentoring. If you and your spouse choose to invest in a new couple, you will bless their fledgling marriage in ways you will never even know. And you will be blessed in a boomerang fashion yourselves.

What you bring from your own seasoned years of marriage is a plethora of practical insights that are often beyond the reach of the more-or-less perfunctory counseling sessions most couples experience (or don't) before marriage. Who you are and what you know are of tremendous value to engaged couples and newlyweds.

This Participant's Guide, along with accompanying video segments, and your instructor will introduce you to the fine art of marriage mentoring, help you assess your personal qualities as a mentor couple, provide you with the tools you need to be effective, and set you up for a series of productive sessions with a newly married or engaged couple.

As marriage mentors, you are the sleeping giant within the church, about to rise and offer immeasurable hope and help to the next generation of married couples. May God bless you as you learn and grow though these materials.

Les and Leslie Parrott
Center for Relationship Development
Seattle Pacific University

WHAT MARRIAGE MENTORING IS AND ISN'T

Overview

In this session you will

1. Rediscover the lost art of mentoring

2. Explore the desperate need for marriage mentoring

3. Define what marriage mentoring is

4. Identify what marriage mentoring is not

The Lost Art of Mentoring

Throughout human history, mentoring has been the primary means of passing on _____ and _____ in every field and in every culture.

The Bible is filled with examples of mentoring. They include:

- Eli and _____

- Elijah and _____

- Moses and _____

- Naomi and _____

- Elizabeth and _____

- Barnabas and _____

- Paul and _____

Into the Word:
Biblical Examples of Mentoring

Directions

1. In this session, you learned that the Bible provides several examples of mentoring relationships. From the list of mentoring relationships below, select one and turn to it in the Scriptures.

   Eli and Samuel (1 Sam. 1–3)

   Elijah and Elisha (1 Kings 19:19–21)

   Moses and Joshua (Deut. 31; Josh. 1)

   Naomi and Ruth (Ruth 1)

   Elizabeth and Mary (Luke 1:39–56)

   Barnabas and Paul (Acts 13–15)

   Paul and Timothy (Acts 16:1–5; 1 Tim. 4; 6:11–20)

2. After reading about the relationship you chose, what qualities do you think made it successful?

The Desperate Need for Marriage Mentoring

- In the 1930s, one out of _____ marriages ended in divorce.

- In the 1960s, it was one out of _____.

- Of the 2.4 million couples who will get married this year in the United States, it is predicted that at least _____ percent will not survive.

- More than _____ new marriages each year end prior to the couple's second anniversary.

The truth is, most engaged couples prepare more for

their_____ than they do for their _____.
Planning the perfect wedding too often takes precedence over planning a successful marriage.

Your Turn:
Personal Mentoring

Directions

1. Before discussing your answers with your partner, take several minutes to think about and answer the questions below.

2. When you have completed the questions, take turns telling your partner about your mentor, the qualities that made him or her a good mentor, and one quality you saw in your mentor you would like to cultivate in yourself.

Have you ever had a mentor? Even if you have not had a mentor in a formal sense, you probably had someone who helped you chart your course and encouraged you along the way.

Who was this person?

How did the mentoring relationship begin?

Use the space below to note several traits this person possessed, qualities that helped him or her be a good mentor to you.

Review your list and circle the one trait you most admired in this person, a trait, perhaps, that would help you as a mentor to newlyweds.

What can you do, at a practical level, to cultivate this quality within yourself?

What Is Marriage Mentoring?

The following list summarizes some of the most important activities a mentor does:

- Mentors give timely _____ to mentorees.

- Mentors _____ various aspects of what they wish to impart.

- Mentors _____ and _____ mentorees to move to higher levels.

- Mentors direct mentorees to helpful _____ when needed.

- Mentors _____ goodness and _____ greatness.

- Mentors lessen a mentoree's anxiety by _____ experiences.

- Mentors help mentorees set _____ and keep them _____ to those goals.

- Mentors provide a periodic _____ and _____ of a mentoree's performance.

Caution: Mentors can do all of the things mentioned above and still not be _____ .

Dynamics of a
Successful Mentoring Relationship

Two dynamics are vital to the success of any mentoring relationship. Without them, all the modeling, challenging, encouraging, goal setting, accountability, and so on, will fall flat. The two critical dynamics

are _____ and _____ .

Definition: A marriage mentor is a _____ , more

_____ couple who _____ a newly married

couple through sharing _____ and

_____ .

Your Turn:
Exploring Your Natural Role

Directions

1. While every marriage mentoring relationship has its own style that unfolds as the relationship develops, some potential confusion can be spared on both sides if the mentors and mentorees discuss their initial expectations of the relationship. This kind of discussion, of course, necessitates that you be clear on your mentoring style before meeting with your mentorees.

2. Think for a moment about how you see yourself as a mentor. Which of the following roles are you and your partner most likely to fall into? Rank the four roles (1 being the most likely), and compare your rankings with your spouse.

We are most naturally inclined to be married mentors that serve as . . .

_____ models   _____ coaches   _____teachers   _____guides

Do your rankings line up with your partners? If not, what does this tell you about what you will be bringing to a mentoring relationship? If your roles differ, how will you complement each other's roles as mentors and what things might you need to be cautious about?

Are there other mentoring roles that come to mind besides the four mentioned here? If so, what are they and how will they impact your mentoring relationship?

What Marriage Mentoring Is Not

It is important to realize exactly what a mentor is not. The following is a list of common mentoring pitfalls. Look to them as a guide to keeping you from making the same mistakes:

• A mentor is not a _____ or _____.

• A mentor is not automatically a _____ or a _____.

• A mentor is not "on call" for every little crisis. His or her time

   is limited to discussion about _____ situations,

   not _____ ones.

• A mentor is not committed _____. The association
   has a natural cycle of its own, not always predictable.

• A mentor is not a _____.

• A mentor is not a _____.

Remember the definition: A mentor is a happy, more experienced couple who empowers a newly married couple through sharing resources and relational experiences.

Summary

In this session you

- Rediscovered the lost art of mentoring
- Explored the desperate need for marriage mentoring
- Defined what marriage mentoring is
- Defined what marriage mentoring is not

ARE YOU FIT TO BE A MARRIAGE MENTOR?

Overview

In this session you will

1. Identify the most important factor in marriage mentoring

2. Assess your own marital fitness for potential mentoring

3. Reflect on three essential qualities for marriage mentoring

What Matters Most

• Each of us is in a relationship with our _____ .

• The single most important factor in effective marriage
  mentoring is who _____ are as a _____
  and as a _____ .

• Regardless of your _____ , _____ , or natural
  _____ , if you do not bring certain
  _____ to the mentoring relationship, there will
  be little chance of it being successful.

Your Turn:
The Marriage Mentoring Self-Test

The following inventory can help determine the degree to which you possess some important traits needed for marriage mentoring.

Directions

1. For each statement below, indicate the response that best identifies your beliefs and attitudes. Keep in mind that the "right" answer is the one that best expresses your thoughts at this time. Use the following code:

   5 = I strongly agree

   4 = I agree

   3 = I am undecided

   2 = I disagree

   1 = I strongly disagree

2. Total your responses to determine the degree to which you have the qualities necessary to be an effective mentor.

_____ 1. Giving advice has little to do with good mentoring.

_____ 2. I can accept and respect people who disagree with me.

_____ 3. I can make a mistake and admit it.

_____ 4. I look at everybody's side of a disagreement before I make a decision.

_____ 5. I project a sense of personal warmth, empathy, and compassion.

_____ 6. I don't need to see immediate and concrete results in order to know progress is occurring.

_____ 7. The personal qualities I possess as a mentor are more important than the skills I use as a mentor.

_____ 8. People believe I am a sincere person.

_____ 9. I have a joyful marriage that I want to share with others.

_____ 10. I know my limits when it comes to helping others.

_____ *Total Score*

Total your responses to determine the degree to which you have the qualities necessary to be an effective mentor:

40–50—You are well on your way to being an effective mentor; take special care to maintain the qualities you have.

30–39—You have what it takes to be effective, but you will need to exert special attention to grooming the traits described in this session.

Below 30—Seek out others' advice and counsel to assess your strengths more accurately.

This quick self-assessment is obviously a simple tool for helping you think about issues important to marriage mentoring. Your instructor or coordinator may have already given you a more objective and thorough assessment, such as the Dyadic Adjustment Scale or the Marital Assessment Inventory, that can protect you and your potential mentorees from an unhealthy situation. One of the most helpful and thorough assessments is called ENRICH, which is similar to PREPARE (both of these tests are described in the Appendix to this guide). It is essential that you take ENRICH if you are going to be using PREPARE with your mentorees. Ask your instructor about taking this valuable inventory.

Essential Traits
of an Effective Mentor: Warmth

• Mentors who possess warmth bring a sense of

  _____ and _____ to the relationship.

• They have an attitude that does not _____ or

  _____ . They may not approve of everything their
  mentorees do, but they still accept them as persons.

• Warmth is not a smothering sentimentality; it simply allows a

  mentor to _____ a mentoree and treat him or her as

  a person of _____ .

• Personal warmth from a mentor _____ mentorees

  from trying to win _____ . Without a generous
  supply of warmth, some mentoree couples will simply perform
  in order to get approval and win their mentor's acceptance—
  never getting the help they really need.

Your Turn:
The Power of Personal Warmth

Directions

Take turns reading and discussing the questions below. Appoint one person in your group to keep track of the time, so that everyone gets a turn.

1. Everyone knows what its like to come into a person's home or office that is not emotionally warm. The lack of acceptance creates an almost physical drop in temperature. Can you think of an example of this kind of experience with a "cold" person from your own life?

2. In comparison, think of a person you know who exudes personal warmth. How do you feel when you are around this person? What happens to your guardedness or defensiveness when you are with him or her?

3. Paul Tournier, the renowned Swiss counselor, said, "I have no methods. All I do is accept people." What do you think this learned and skilled Christian counselor meant by this statement, and how can it apply to cultivating personal warmth in marriage mentoring?

Essential Traits
of an Effective Mentor: Genuineness

• Genuineness cannot be _____ . Either you

_____ want to help or you are simply playing the

sterile _____ of a mentor, hiding behind masks,

defenses, or facades. In other words, genuineness is something

you _____ , not something you _____ .

• Genuineness has been described as a _____ to the
heart. Jesus said, "Blessed are the pure in heart." Or to put it
another way, "Consider the mentor in whom there is no guile."

• When genuineness is present, a _____ and

even _____ mentoree couple is likely to

_____ with you and invest _____
in the mentoring process.

Essential Traits
of an Effective Mentor: Empathy

- Empathy lets your mentorees know you _____ their

  words, _____ their thoughts, and _____
  their feelings. This does not mean you necessarily understand all
  that is going on for them, but it does mean you understand
  what they feel and think.

- Empathy is more than feeling a mentoree couple's feelings; it is

  also being _____ enough to not allow your feelings
  to blend with theirs.

Into the Word:
What the Bible says about Empathy

Directions

Marriage mentors can learn much from what the Bible has to say about the important quality of empathy. Discuss the questions listed below, taking special care to allow everyone a chance to give their input.

1. Read Philippians 2:3–8. Who was the greatest example of empathy ever? Why?

2. Empathy is not easy. Read Luke 22:39–44. How have you found empathy to be hard work in your own life?

3. Read Luke 7:11–15. How is the story of Jesus and the widow at Nain a good biblical example of empathy?

Summary

In this session you

- Identified the most important factor in marriage mentoring
- Assessed your own marital fitness for potential mentoring
- Reflected on three essential qualities for marriage mentoring

A TOOLBOX FOR MARRIAGE MENTORS

Overview

In this session you will

1. Discover you don't have to be a marriage expert to be a marriage mentor

2. Master the skills of clarifying content and reflecting feeling

3. Learn why giving advice so often fails

You Don't Have to Be a Marriage Expert

The fundamental skill of marriage mentoring can be summed up in a single word: _____ .

_____ listening—listening with "the _____ ear" as psychologist and author Theodor Reik called it—is the _____ of effective marriage mentoring.

Two major ingredients go into active listening:

1. Clarifying _____

2. Reflecting _____

Into the Word:
Biblical Examples of Listening

Directions

1. There are more than two hundred occurrences of the word *listen* in the Bible. Look up a couple of the Scriptures listed below and take a few minutes to discover what they have to say about listening.

- Luke 2:46

- Acts 26:3

- James 1:19

- Proverbs 18:13

Skill-Builder One: Clarifying Content

Love

isnowhere

• In mentoring another couple, being misunderstood is no

  _____ matter.

• Misunderstanding does not come because we do not

  _____ the words a person is saying, but because we

  do not _____ the meaning of the words.

• For the _____ most commonly used words in the

  English language, there are over _____ different
  meanings. This means that, on average, there are about

  _____ different meanings for _____
  of the words we most commonly use.

Your Turn: Clarifying Content

Directions

1. Following are some typical newlywed statements. Read each separately and clarify its meaning.

2. In the space below each statement, write out a response that clarifies its content as if you were actually listening to, summarizing, and clarifying that statement.

3. Compare your list of reflective statements to those listed on the next page to see how accurately you clarify content and recognize feelings. Give yourself a 2 on those items where your choice closely matches, a 1 on items where your choice only partially matches, and a 0 if you missed altogether. Total your score and rate your ability to clarify content using the table at the bottom of that page.

"We work at communication skills all the time, but it doesn't make any difference."

"Every other couple seemed to get an invitation but us."

"Sometimes I feel myself biting my tongue when I'd really like to tell him how upset I am."

"If we aren't getting anywhere on an issue, I just need to take a timeout. I mean, what's the use?"

"Sometimes I feel like I am living out a fairy tale. I never dreamed marriage would be so great."

"I don't feel anything about it."

Answers

"We work at communication skills all the time, but it doesn't make any difference."
—*So you are working on trying to improve.*

"Every other couple seemed to get an invitation but us."
—*Are you saying you were left out on purpose?*

"Sometimes I feel myself biting my tongue when I'd really like to tell him how upset I am."
—*You consciously hold back what you would like to say?*

"If we aren't getting anywhere on an issue, I just need to take a time-out. I mean, what's the use?"
—*Are you saying that you want to either make progress right now or simply set the issue aside?*

"Sometimes I feel like I am living out a fairy tale. I never dreamed marriage would be so great."
—*Sounds like marriage is better than you thought it would be.*

"I don't feel anything about it."
—*You truthfully are apathetic?*

How you rate on clarifying content:

    10–12 Above average

    6–9   Average

    0–5   Below average

Skill-Builder Two:
Reflecting Feelings

- Understanding comes through reflecting another person's

  feelings—responding sensitively to the _____ rather

  than the _____ meaning of a person's expression.

- You can reflect another's feelings and be dead _____ ,

  but still _____ as a marriage mentor. Why?

  Because as long as you are genuinely _____ to
  understand what someone is feeling (and reflecting it), that person feels more understood. You can't fail as long as you are genuinely trying!

- Just as a mirror reflects an image of the person looking into it

  and helps them define their _____ , so reflecting the
  emotions of another person helps them define their

  _____ .

- Between what a person _____ to communicate and what

  others hear stands an unavoidable filter of _____ .

Your Turn:
Reflecting Feelings

Directions

1. Important feelings are often hidden behind the words of a new-lywed. Following are the same statements you used to clarify content. This time, read each separately and listen for feelings.

2. Make note of the feeling you hear and write out a response that reflects that feeling for each of the statements.

3. Compare your list of reflective statements to those listed on page 40 to see how accurately you reflect feelings. Give yourself a 2 on those items where your choice closely matches, a 1 on items where your choice only partially matches, and a 0 if you missed altogether. Total your score and rate your ability to clarify content using the table at the bottom of that page.

"We work at communication skills all the time, but it doesn't make any difference."

"Every other couple seemed to get an invitation but us."

"Sometimes I feel myself biting my tongue when I'd really like to tell him how upset I am."

"If we aren't getting anywhere on an issue, I just need to take a time-out. I mean, what's the use?"

"Sometimes I feel like I am living out a fairy tale. I never dreamed marriage would be so great."

"I don't feel anything about it."

Answers

"We work at communication skills all the time, but it doesn't make any difference."
—*Sounds like you feel discouraged.*

"Every other couple seemed to get an invitation but us."
—*It sounds kind of like you feel left out.*

"Sometimes I feel myself biting my tongue when I'd really like to tell him how upset I am."
—*You feel really angry at times.*

"If we aren't getting anywhere on an issue, I just need to take a time-out. I mean, what's the use?"
—*As you say that I get a picture of a guy who is discouraged and is crying uncle.*

"Sometimes I feel like I am living out a fairy tale. I never dreamed marriage would be so great."
—*Sounds like you couldn't feel happier.*

"I don't feel anything about it."
—*I'm wondering if you have some idea of what you should be feeling and because you are not, you register it as not feeling anything.*

How you rate on reflecting feelings:

    10–12 Above average

    6–9   Average

    0–5   Below average

Why Giving Advice So Often Fails

- While giving advice may be part of the process, the mentors' main

   job is to _____ a relationship, to _____

   understanding, and to help newlyweds _____ the
   resources they need.

- Advice is often _____.

- Advice can make a couple feel _____.

- Advice can be _____.

- Advice can be _____.

Summary

In this session you

• Discovered you don't have to be a marriage expert to be a marriage mentor

• Mastered the skills of clarifying content and reflecting feeling

• Learned why giving advice so often fails

QUESTIONS ENGAGED AND NEWLYWED COUPLES ASK

Overview

In this session you will

1. Discover you know more than you think you do

2. Learn that your story is your answer

3. Find out where to turn when you don't have the answer

What Your Mentorees Expect of You

- Most newly married couples come into marriage with dozens

  of _____ questions—and in many cases, they

  don't even know the questions to ask until _____
  they get married.

- Your newlyweds won't _____ you to have the
  answer for every question they ask.

Your Turn: Giving It Your Best Shot

Directions

1. Take a moment to answer the following questions a newlywed might ask. Don't try to be a know-it-all; just be authentic.

2. Write your response in the place provided. If you don't have any idea, just leave it blank.

How can I be honest without hurting my partner's feelings?

What should we do when we can't agree?

How do we find time for each other amidst our busy schedules?

Why do I sometimes still feel lonely?

Do men and woman communicate differently?

What if my in-laws smother us?

Should we have separate bank accounts?

What if my partner's personality changes after we get married?

What can we do if our sex drives differ?

How can we have a consistent and meaningful devotional time together?

How Your Story is Your Answer

Categories of marital questions:

- _____

- _____

- _____

- _____

- _____

- _____

- _____

- _____

- _____

- _____

- As you attempted to answer the questions in the "Your Turn" exercise, you probably had a few where you really did not have much more information than your own _____ .

- If you are willing to be a little _____ with your couple, you can help them find the answers to their questions, whether you have them or not.

- Your story gives them something to _____ to, either in agreement or disagreement. Either way, you have helped them _____ the issue.

Your Turn: Where Do You Need to Brush Up?

Directions

1. Earlier in this session you learned about the most common categories of questions newlyweds have. Review the list again and rank the three or four with which you feel most knowledgeable and thus most comfortable in discussing. Place a one (1) next to the category in which you are most confident, then a two (2), and so on.

2. Next, rank the three or four categories in which you feel least confident, those areas where you don't feel you have the best information. Place a letter "A" next to the category with which you feel the least comfortable, then "B," and so on.

_____ Communication

_____ Conflict

_____ Careers

_____ Emotions

_____ Gender

_____ In-laws

_____ Intimacy

_____ Money

_____ Personality

_____ Sex

_____ Spiritual matters

Where to Turn
When You Don't Know the Answer

There will be times when your story is not _____

or is no substitute for _____ information.

- What do we do if _____ is a repetitive problem?

- Should we never keep a _____ from each other?

- What happens when a _____ works outside the home?

- How do we get out of _____ ?

- How do we start a _____ and stick to it?

- What should _____ know about a woman's menstrual cycle?

- How many times does the average couple have

  _____ in a month?

- What if one of us has been sexually _____ in our past?

- What if my spouse is not a _____ ?

- You could go to a public _____ or a

  _____ to hunt for a resource that might help.

- We recommend a straight shooting little reference guide called

  _____ (Zondervan).

- The _____ of your Participant's Guide contains an annotated list of resources.

Into the Word:
What the Bible Has to Say about Marriage

Directions

Some newlyweds are very motivated to learn what the Bible has to say about marriage, but many become discouraged because they do not discover Scripture's practical information for couples.

1. Below is a small sampling of various verses that address marriage. Choose at least five of the passages, read them aloud within your group, and discuss.

   Mark 10:8–9

   Colossians 3:19

   Proverbs 12:4

   Mark 10:6

   Ephesians 5:25–26

   Proverbs 18:13

   Ephesians 5:28

   Proverbs 17:14

   1 Corinthians 7:4

   1 Corinthians 13:6–7

   Hebrews 13:4

   Proverbs 19:13

   1 Timothy 3:11

   Matthew 7:12

   1 Peter 3:7

   Mark 10:7–8

   Proverbs 21:14

Summary

In this session you

- Discovered you know more than you think you do
- Learned that your story is your answer
- Found out where to turn when you don't have the answer

THE FIRST MENTOR MEETING WITH YOUR COUPLE

Overview

In this session you will

1. Learn the best way to make contact with your mentor couple

2. Focus on to what to talk about

3. Find out how to use *Marriage Partnership* magazine and *Saving Your Marriage Before It Starts*

4. Learn more about setting subsequent meetings and what to discuss in them

5. Explore mentoring between meetings

Making Contact

- The very first contact you have with your mentoree couple may

    occur over the _____ , by _____ ,

    or in _____ .

- _____ should not be in short supply.

- The pragmatic goal of the first contact is to set a _____
  for the four of you to get together. It is important to make

    _____ arrangements for your meeting.

- While it is great to invite them into your _____
  for a meal or a snack, it may be more simple to meet at a

    _____ for a cup of coffee. The goal it not to

    _____ , but to mentor.

What to Talk About

Your first meeting is more a time of getting _____ than anything else.

In addition to getting to know your mentorees, this first session should also focus on the couple's personal _____ for marriage.

• What _____ of marriage do they want to build?

• What marriages have they seen that they _____ and why?

• What _____ , patterns, behaviors, and rituals do they want to incorporate into their marriage?

Your Turn: Setting Marriage Goals

Directions

1. In exploring you mentoree's goals for marriage, you may want to have them write down their ideas in specific terms. You may even want to have them do this before getting together for your first session. This will help the mentoree couple prepare for your time together and give you some concrete information to explore.

   You might write something like this: "One of the most important yet least talked about domains of marriage is the vision you share for your first year together. Take a moment to discuss what you hope to achieve (i.e., your goals) as a couple. What would you like to accomplish at three months, at seven months, and at one year? Consider communication and conflict, spirituality, intimacy, financial management, outside relationships, traditions for holidays, and so on. Be as specific as possible." Then have them write their goals for after three months, seven months, and twelve months of marriage.

2. Before you have your couple do this however, pretend you could start your own marriage over. Discuss and write down what your own three-, seven-, and twelve-month goals would be in the space provided below.

Three-month goal:

Seven-month goal:

Twelve-month goal:

Using *Marriage Partnership* Magazine

• It provides a common _____ point for discussing a variety of topics in a nonthreatening way.

• Use it to raise issues you feel are _____ for your couple to discuss.

As a part of this *Mentoring Engaged and Newlywed Couples* curriculum, you are eligible to receive discounted subscriptions to the magazine. For a limited time, you can save $5.00 on this exceptional marriage resource! Regularly priced at $19.95, this special offer allows you to try *Marriage Partnership* magazine for only $14.95. You may wish to contact the magazine directly at:

Marriage Partnership
Christianity Today, Inc.
465 Gundersen Drive
Carol Stream, IL 60188
Or call: 1-800-627-4942

When calling or writing, ask for special offer #E7C01.

Using *Saving Your Marriage Before It Starts*

The book is built around the following seven questions:

1. Have you faced the _____ of marriage with honesty?

2. Can you identify your _____ style?

3. Have you developed the habit of _____ ?

4. Can you say what you mean and _____ what you hear?

5. Have you bridged the _____ gap?

6. Do you know how to _____ a good fight?

7. Are you and your partner _____ mates?

Where Do We Go from Here?

Before concluding your first meeting you will want to talk about and

_____ your next time together. It is important to have

a _____ date on the calendar that both your and your
couple can look forward to and count on.

In subsequent sessions, you will want to address the following
topics:

- Setting up a new _____ together

- Agreeing on _____ management

- Negotiating _____ roles

- Managing _____

- Dealing with _____ relations

- Preparing for _____

- Coping with _____ issues

- Cultivating _____ intimacy

- Celebrating _____ and married life

Your Turn: Mentoring in Secret

Directions

One of the best ways for any couple to grow closer together is to reach out to others as a team, to meet the needs of others not as individuals but as a couple. What is even better is to do this in secret!

1. Brainstorm with your partner how you could do something for your mentor couple that they would never even know you did. Of course, this is easier once you have already become acquainted with your mentorees and discovered some of their unique needs and desires. But for now, write down two or three ways the two of you could do some shared service in secret.

Mentoring Between Meetings

- Keep your couple's _____ (along with their phone number and address) posted in a convenient location. This will help you keep them in mind, pray for them, and make it easier to send them mail or make a call.

- Mail a note of _____ to your couple from time to time. Even a brief card saying that you are thinking of them can be a real uplift.

- Send your couple a helpful _____ about marriage you have read. Simply clip it out, write a quick note on it, and drop it in an envelope to them.

- With the _____ of your mentorees, make contact with their parents. Let their parents know of your mentoring relationship and how you enjoy their children.

- Let your couple know about an upcoming marriage

  _____ or a guest speaker (at your church or a community function).

- Send your couple a few _____ for things they might use. Simply clip coupons for various products over a few days and send them to your couple.

- Invite your couple to your _____ if they are looking for a new church home.

- Let your couple know about an upcoming _____ news show that has a segment about marriage.

- Invite your couple into your _____ for a meal or dessert.

- Send your couple a _____ card with a personal note about how you will be thinking of them during the holiday season.

- "Allow" your couple to _____ your kids. (This is an activity that many newlyweds enjoy as they think about their future family).

- Send your couple an _____ card. Do this not just on their first anniversary, but for years that follow. This is a special way of staying in touch. After all, how many anniversary cards do you receive?

Into the Word:
The Boomerang Effect of Mentoring

Directions

In the first session you learned that the Bible provides several examples of mentoring relationships. You learned about Eli and Samuel, Elijah and Elisha, Moses and Joshua, Naomi and Ruth, Elizabeth and Mary, Barnabas and Paul, Paul and Timothy.

1. Review your notes from that first session and visit once again Scripture examples of mentoring. Then explore how in many cases the mentor received just as much of a blessing from the relationship as the mentorees did. Record your notes in the space provided.

Summary

In this session you

- Learned the best way to make contact with your mentor couple

- Focused on what to talk about

- Found out how to use *Marriage Partnership* magazine and *Saving Your Marriage Before It Starts*

- Learned more about setting subsequent meetings and what to discuss in them

- Explored mentoring between meetings

APPENDIX

AN IMPORTANT
MESSAGE FOR
PREWEDDING
MENTORS

If you are mentoring engaged couples—versus newlyweds—you must take special care in being particularly knowledgeable of premarriage issues. Ideally, you will be working in concert with a counselor or minister, augmenting his or her programmed approach.

Be aware of the fact that many experienced premarriage counselors will administer an important assessment called PREPARE (*Pre*marital *Pe*rsonal *a*nd *R*elationship *E*valuation). Designed by former president of the National Council on Family Relations Dr. David Olson, it is the most widely administered premarital instrument in the United States. It consists of 125 questions (categorized upon tabulation into ten crucial areas), takes about thirty minutes, and does an excellent job at helping seriously-dating or engaged couples evaluate their relationship. It is well designed and easily administered.

Individuals are asked if they "Agree Strongly," "Agree," or if they are "Undecided," "Disagree," or "Disagree Strongly" with random statements like these:

- I believe that most disagreements we currently have will decrease after marriage.
- I really like the personality and habits of my partner.
- I can easily share my positive and negative feelings with my partner.
- I wish my partner were more careful in spending money.

A thirty-dollar fee per couple is charged for questionnaire evaluation. The questionnaires (taken by each individual in the couple) are compared anonymously by computer and a report is sent to the pastor or counselor who administered the questionnaire. The couple then meets with the counselor for two or more feedback sessions to review the strengths and "growth areas" of their relationship.

Each engaged couple is given a pamphlet, "Building a Strong Marriage," which emphasizes that PREPARE is "not a test. No one passes or fails." It is simply designed to make couples more aware of their strengths and the areas where they will need to work for growth.

Why is an assessment like this important? Remarkably, PREPARE can predict with astonishing accuracy which couples will divorce. A study by Blaine Fowers of 148 couples who took PREPARE in 1980 and were contacted two years later showed very impressive results. "Using PREPARE scores . . . it was possible to predict with 86% accuracy those couples that eventually got divorced and with 78% accuracy those couples who were happily married," said the Fowers study. The average prediction rate for both groups was 81%. What's more, a tenth of those who take PREPARE decide not to marry. In other words, taking the assessment and receiving feedback on the results serves an extremely important preventive function by helping some couples decide not to marry if they have a high probability of facing divorce.

Most likely, there are pastors and counselors in your community who are trained to administer PREPARE. Some twenty thousand instructors have been trained nationally. If you would like to locate such a counselor, write PREPARE/ENRICH, P.O. Box 190, Minneapolis, MN 55440–0190.

If you are interested in being trained to administer and interpret PREPARE yourself, ask that your pastor (or an area counselor) contact PREPARE at the same address and arrange a time for you and other couples in your church or area to be trained.

Training is a simple two-step process. First, you and your spouse take the ENRICH questionnaire (for already married couples) to get an idea of what you will be asking your mentorees to do. Second, you will attend a six-hour training session on a Saturday in which an expert will teach you how to interpret the PREPARE computer report for each couple with whom you are working. It's that easy—and inexpressibly important.

For a more complete description of PREPARE and many other important aspects of mentoring engaged couples, you will want to read Michael J. McManus's excellent book, *Marriage Savers: Helping Your Friends and Family Stay Married* (Zondervan, 1993). This book is a "must read" for marriage mentors.

RESOURCES FOR MARRIAGE MENTORS

The following list of resources is not exhaustive. It is simply designed to serve as a springboard for finding some books in a particular area that may help you better mentor engaged and newlywed couples.

Communication

Men Are From Mars, Women Are From Venus: A Practical Guide for Improving Communication and Getting What You Want in Your Relationship by John Gray (HarperCollins, 1992).

Using the metaphor of Martians and Venusians attempting to communicate, John Gray illustrates commonly occurring conflicts between men and women when trying to communicate. This wildly popular book explains how differences can come between the sexes and prohibit mutually fulfilling loving relationships.

How to Talk So Your Mate Will Listen and Listen So Your Mate Will Talk by Nancy L. Van Pelt (Revell, 1989).

This book presents a variety of techniques and strategies for developing skills to establish and sustain healthy communication. Among the topics are: listening through nonverbals, creative questioning, marital bonding, and his and her talk styles. Each chapter is integrated with spiritual understanding and biblical principles.

Communication: Key to Your Marriage by H. Norman Wright (Regal, 1974).

A classic in many ways, this book has taught many couples over the years the fundamentals to good communication. It contains ten practical principles for building your partner's self-esteem, ten methods for handling angry feelings, ten steps to avoiding worry, and so on. This one is chock-full of guidelines you can use to enrich and deepen your communication.

Conflict

Why Marriages Succeed or Fail by John Gottman (Simon & Schuster, 1994).

Based on a study of more than two thousand married couples over two decades, this book pinpoints just what makes marriage work. According to the author, the most serious threats to a lasting marriage are found in how a couple handles conflict. With lucid examples and self-tests, this book will help you spot potential problem patterns in your own marriage and guide you to healthier ways of interacting.

We Can Work It Out: Making Sense of Marital Conflict by Clifford Notarious and
    Howard Markman (Putman, 1993).

The key to a happy and successful marriage, according to these authors, relies on a couple's ability to handle their differences, not on whom each chooses for a mate. Based on ground-breaking research, they offer an innovative three-part communication program designed to defuse any argument. With questionnaires, exercises, and anecdotes, *We Can Work It Out* is a refreshingly optimistic guide-book to resolving conflict.

*Fighting for Your Marriage: Positive Steps for Preventing Divorce and Preserving a
    Lasting Love* by Howard Markman, Scott Stanley, and Susan L. Blumberg
    (Jossey-Bass Publishers, 1994).

These authors bring a dauntless optimism to making marriage work. Their book is based on the highly praised PREP (Prevention and Relationship Enhancement Program) workshop and demonstrates the kinds of techniques that have proven effective for preventing marital problems. They show how men and women differ in the way they fight and seek intimacy in marriage, why adding structure to conversation can help keep hot topics from turning into marital meltdowns, and so on.

Careers

How to Work With the One You Love and Live to Tell About It by Cameron and
    Donna Partow (Bethany House, 1995).

If you work in the same company, volunteer on the same committees, or put up wallpaper together, this book lays out the potential problems and helps you solve them before they get serious. The Partows show you how to evaluate the pros and cons of working together, manage risk, build accountability without nagging or dominating, and resolve conflict. If you work together or plan to, this one is worth a look.

Winning at Work Without Losing at Love by Stephen Arterburn (Nelson, 1994).

Some people sacrifice just about anything for career success. Others focus exclusively on their relationships and have a difficult time making ends meet. Arterburn believes you don't have to have one without the other—you can be a winner in both business and marriage. He shows you how to establish a solid foundation for success at work and at home, and he teaches you how to set achievable goals that create a win/win situation for everyone.

Achieving Success Without Failing Your Family by Paul Faulkner (Howard Publishing, 1994).

Some experts say you cannot have both career success and family excellence. This book proves them wrong. It is the story of thirty families who have practiced proven strategies for building successful careers and strong families. Through their examples, you will learn the importance of family traditions, the principle of being intentional, and so on. This book is particularly relevant when children become part of your home.

The Career Counselor by Leslie and Les Parrott (Word, 1995).

Written for people who are serious about charting their lifelong career path and staying afloat in today's rapidly changing job market, this book notes four mistakes to avoid in any career decision, sure-fire ways to assess and market your own job skills, seven keys to bouncing back from a crushing job loss, and practical ways to snap the paralysis of indecision.

Emotions

Unlocking the Mystery of Your Emotions by Archibald Hart (Word, 1989).

Many people either lose control of their emotions (creating pain and chaos) or over-control them (becoming stunted, distant, and cold). This book shows you how to experience emotions fully without letting them get out of hand. With balanced professionalism, biblical integrity, and down-to-earth practicality, Dr. Hart shows how you can learn to be "real" instead of perfect.

Love's Unseen Enemy: How to Overcome Guilt to Build Healthy Relationships by Les Parrott III (Zondervan, 1994).

Too often efforts to build a loving marriage are unwittingly sabotaged by an unseen enemy: guilt. This book shows how to build a healthy relationship by overcoming feelings of false guilt and by dealing forthrightly with true guilt. It identifies four relationship styles created by the combination of love and guilt: Pleaser, Controller, Withholder, and Lover.

Love and Anger in Marriage by David Mace (Zondervan, 1982).

World-renowned marriage counselor David Mace believes that many people have totally overlooked the positive functions anger can perform for them—even in close, intimate relationships like marriage. Mace demonstrates the interaction that takes place between a couple as their relationship grows and develops through the many love-anger cycles that arise in daily living together. This honest book will bring new life and hope to many angry marriages.

Gender

His Needs Her Needs: Building an Affair-proof Marriage by Willard F. Harley Jr. (Fleming Revel, 1986).

Harley writes with conviction that couples need to learn how to care for each other by understanding fundamental gender differences. Once a spouse understands his or her partner's unique needs, the process of trying to meet those needs can begin. Harley shows you how to become "irresistible" to each other and avoid the common errors that lead to affairs and divorce.

Men & Women: Enjoying the Difference by Larry Crabb (Zondervan, 1991).

Giving numerous examples from his counseling and speaking ministry, Crabb explores how we can turn away from ourselves and toward each other, and how we can consider our mate's needs and become what he calls "othercentered." He maintains that men and women are different in important ways that, if understood and honored, can lead to a deep enjoyment of one another, an enjoyment that can last forever.

You Just Don't Understand: Women and Men in Conversation by Deborah Tannen (Ballantine, 1990).

A professor of linguistics, Dr. Tannen provides a readable account of the complexities of communication between men and women. What she is saying is that men and women grow up in such profoundly different ways and see themselves connecting to others in such profoundly different ways that the two sexes are really trying to communicate across two different cultures. This book goes a long way toward helping couples speak the same language.

How to Change Your Spouse (Without Ruining Your Marriage) by H. Norman Wright and Gary J. Oliver (Servant, 1994).

This book offers scores of life-changing insights gleaned from professional marriage therapists and couples who desperately wanted to improve their marriages. As the authors explain gender differences, you will learn how to effectively bring about the changes you long for in your partner so that your marriage can blossom like you want it to.

In-laws

Mothers, Sons and Wives by H. Norman Wright (Regal, 1994).

It should be no surprise that the powerful bond between a mother and son puts pressure on many marriages. "When a man's relationship with his mother is so powerful," asks Norm Wright, "is there any room for his wife?" This book is dedicated to helping wives find peace in the midst of the mother-son-wife triangle. It takes a close look at this in-law relationship and helps couples establish healthy boundaries as well as open lines of communication. Read it and make peace with "the other woman."

Boundaries: When to Say Yes, When to Say No, To Take Control of Your Life by Henry Cloud and John Townsend (Zondervan, 1992).

Having clear boundaries is essential to a healthy relationship with in-laws. A boundary is a personal property line that marks those things for which we are responsible. In other words, boundaries define who we are. In this best-selling book, Cloud and Townsend describe the importance of physical, mental, emotional, and spiritual boundaries. While this book is not written solely about setting boundaries with in-laws, many of its principles can be applied to this relationship.

In-laws, Outlaws: How to Make Peace With His Family and Yours by P. Bilosfsky and F. Sacharow (Villard, 1991).

This book points the way to skills needed to understand, intercept, and solve nearly every type of in-law problem. Readers learn how to master good interpersonal communication, set limits and boundaries, adjust their own expectations to reality and recognize core issues rather than respond to the immediate situation. With step-by-step instructions, the book addresses issues such as meeting your in-laws for the first time, planning the wedding, when children arrive (or don't), holidays and family gatherings, and reaching out to sibling in-laws.

Intimacy

Holding On to Romance by H. Norman Wright (Regal, 1992).

In this book, marriage expert Norman Wright shows couples how to recapture the elusive feeling of romance and intimacy. He points to the fact that your spouse cannot know you unless you invite him or her into your inner world. But he doesn't just leave you there. He shows you how to cultivate intimacy by speaking your spouse's language and prospering in the midst of a "love recession." The bottom line is that this book walks you through specific things you can do and say to rekindle the passion that first drew you together.

The Intimacy Factor by David Stoop and Jan Stoop (Nelson, 1993).

The Stoops demonstrate how family history, early behavior, birth order, and general home environment all contribute in a profound and critical way to shaping your personality and the way you relate to your spouse. Once you understand these influences and your different personality types, you will be able to build a more intimate relationship with your spouse. According to the Stoops, "intimacy is not a goal in and of itself. It is much like happiness: the more you actively seek it, the more elusive it becomes. Intimacy is a by-product of the right kinds of behaviors."

Intimate Marriage by Charles M. Sell (Multnomah, 1982).

"This book is designed to help the two of you make the most important discovery of all—each other." So writes the author of this helpful book. He points out that individual differences can work for marriage intimacy, not against it. Covering everything from sensuality to conflict, Charles Sell shows you how to cultivate intimacy even when it seems impossible. This is a book built on the conviction that, in spite of negative emotions and differences of opinion, spiritual, emotional, and physical oneness in marriage *is* achievable.

Money

The Christian's Guide to Worry-free Money Management by Daniel B. Busby, Kent
   E. Barber, and Robert L. Temple (Zondervan, 1994).

When it comes to money, the Bible has a lot to say, and it makes it very clear that God expects us to be stewards of the resources entrusted to us. *The Christian's Guide to Worry-free Money Management* explains in a step-by-step fashion how to apply principles of responsible stewardship in your personal finances. It provides a money management system that fulfills God's commandments and frees you from financial worries. Study questions, practical tips, and worksheets in this resource will help you plot a path toward financial security.

The Christian's Guide to Wise Investing by Gary D. Moore (Zondervan, 1994).

Whether you have five hundred or five hundred *thousand* dollars to invest, *The Christian's Guide to Wise Investing* gives you the knowledge you need to be smart with your money. If you have ever experienced confusion from experts' exotic talk about the myriad of financial investment options, rest assured you will not find that in this volume. It is written with a firm footing in biblical principles and in clear, concise language you will understand.

Secrets to Financial Success in Marriage by John C. Shimer (Successful Financial
   Planners, 1993).

Far more than just a manual on banking and budgeting, this book gives couples a larger picture of the importance of money in marriage. It examines such diverse topics as how to talk about dreams and make them come true, the relationship between personal values and money, and so on. This book is not about getting rich; instead, it is about building a happy, prosperous, and balanced partnership.

Other Relationships and Marriage

The Friendship Factor by Alan Loy McGinnis (Augsburg, 1979).

This best-selling book has become a classic on friendship. While it is not particularly for married couples, its principles certainly apply. Topics include: "Five Ways to Deepen Your Relationships," "Five Guidelines for Cultivating Intimacy," "Two Ways to Handle Negative Emotions Without Destroying the Relationship," and "What Happens When Your Relationships Go Bad?" The chapter titled "Eros: Its Power and Its Problems" is particularly helpful to married couples dealing with male-female friendships.

High-Maintenance Relationships: How to Handle Impossible People by Les Parrott III (Tyndale, 1996).

How do we cope with difficult relationships that affect our marriage? When should we love without limits, and when should we love with definite limits? *High-Maintenance Relationships* offers clear and direct answers for dealing with relationships that give so little but demand so much. Each chapter offers vignettes to help readers identify difficult relationships, a self-test to identify people who exemplify the high-maintenance relationship, and extensive coping strategies to deal with difficult people in several settings.

Can Men and Women Be Just Friends? by Andy Bustanoby (Zondervan, 1993).

In this book, Andy Bustanoby helps both men and women understand what friendship is, how to handle opposite-sex friendships, how to know when an outside "friendship" endangers your marriage, and how to make your spouse your best friend. In addition, his "Couples' Friendship Inventory" will help you evaluate the quality of the friendship in your marriage. This book gives clear, pointed advice on how to build strong, godly friendships. Every couple can learn from this one.

Personality

Were You Born for Each Other? by Kevin Leman (Delacorte, 1991).

Birth order expert Dr. Kevin Leman applies his research to the marriage relationship in this book and claims that the secret to romantic happiness doesn't lie in chemistry, timing, or even luck. Leman says the most important factor is birth order. He describes what each birth order—firstborn, middleborn, and lastborn—is like within a marriage. Among other things, he deals with how to cope if your birth orders aren't ideally suited for one another.

Please Understand Me: Character & Temperament Types by David Keirsey and Marilyn Bates (Prometheus Nemesis, 1984).

This is one of the most popular and accessible books for understanding various personality types. You begin by completing a questionnaire (adapted from the Myers-Briggs Type Indicator) to determine which of the sixteen types fits your personality. The book provides a useful vocabulary and phraseology for having a meaningful and productive discussion of how your differences in personality complement one another.

Discover Your Personality Type and How to Get Along With Others by H. Horman Wright and Sheffield (Gospel Light, 1996).

Based on the Myers-Briggs Type Indicator, this complete video seminar with multiple sessions totals 140 minutes. The presentation will help you build better relationships, not just with your spouse, but with everyone. It will show you how different personality types view life and react in a variety of ways. Not only can people learn to understand their differences, but they can value and capitalize on them. This video literally shows you how.

The Intimacy Factor by David and Jan Stoop (Nelson, 1993).

Do you really know what type of personality you have? Or what type your spouse has? Does your personality really affect the intimacy you achieve in a relationship? These are the questions this book answers. Based primarily on the popular Myers-Briggs Type Indicator, it explores the differences between extroverts and introverts, thinking and feeling, judging and perceiving, and so on. All the while, the Stoops show how our personalities affect our ability to love and be loved.

Sexuality

Getting Your Sex Life Off to a Great Start: A Guide for Engaged and Newlywed Couples by Clifford and Joyce Penner (Word, 1994).

Intelligent, deliberate preparation for a lifetime of sexual pleasure is a worthy investment, and this book is an excellent guide to doing just that. Renowned sexual counselors and best-selling authors Cliff and Joyce Penner take you through an encouraging process that begins by dispelling sexual myths and then guiding you in getting to know yourself and each other emotionally and physically. With reassuring enthusiasm and straightforward advice, the Penners show you how to clarify your expectations and pursue true marital passion through creative, step-by-step exercises and easy-to-understand examples.

The Gift of Sex: A Guide to Sexual Fulfillment by Clifford and Joyce Penner (Word, 1981).

This is an ideal guide for understanding your own sexuality and the sexual relationship in marriage with all its pleasure, drive, frustration, and fulfillment. The book focuses on the physical dimension (how our bodies work), the total experince (having fun, pleasuring, stimulating, etc.), moving past sexual barriers (differing sexual needs), resolving technical difficulties (no arousal, pain, etc.), and finding help, all from a thoroughly Christian perspective built on the premise that sexuality is a gift from God. The Penners have included well over a dozen sexual enhancement exercises that have proven helpful to thousands of married couples. The book is readable, practical, frank, and intimate.

A Celebration of Sex: A Christian Couple's Manual by Douglas E. Rosenau (Nelson, 1994).

This thorough book provides assistance on dozens of sexual issues, and answers specific, often unasked questions about sexual topics. It presents all married couples with detailed techniques and behavioral skills for a full awareness and understanding of sexual pleasure needed to deepen intimate companionship. One of the strengths of this volume is the inclusion of several detailed diagrams and illustrations. The goal of *A Celebration of Sex* is to help you create the one-flesh union that God has ordained, the spiritual merger of wife and husband.

The Sexual Man by Archibald D. Hart (Word, 1994).

This is an honest, carefully documented book that answers dozens of questions about today's men and their sexuality. Dr. Hart has surveyed more than six hundred men to discover what satisfies men sexually, what sexual fears and failures haunt them, and the keys to a fulfilled and guilt-free sex life. This book, however, is not for men only. Every wife can learn more about her partner by reading these pages, which are packed with helpful charts depicting characteristics of male sexuality.

Your Wife Was Sexually Abused by John Courtright and Sid Rogers (Zondervan, 1994).

If your wife has been sexually abused, this little book is a must. It points to a healing path through the pain and confusion. Written by two men who have had to deal with past sexual abuse in their own marriages, this book will help you cope. Each heart-moving chapter includes questions for thought and discussion that will help you work through your own personal situation to a healthy and stable marriage.

Spirituality and Marriage

Marriage Spirituality: Ten Disciplines for Couples Who Love God by Paul Stevens (InterVarsity, 1989).

Paul Stevens begins with the premise that we do not have to develop our spirituality alone, as if we were all monks. He presents ten spiritual disciplines that every couple can practice together. From prayer to service, conversation to confession, each of these disciplines strengthens both faith and marriage. In the context of each chapter you will discover not only solid biblical principles, but many practical suggestions as well.

The Spiritually Intimate Marriage: Discover the Close Relationship God Has Designed for Every Couple by Donald Harvey (Fleming Revell, 1991).

Drawing from case studies and his own personal experience to define spiritual intimacy, Donald Harvey identifies problems that inhibit closeness and offers counsel for working with a mate who isn't ready for a deeper level of intimacy. This book will show you how to take the steps necessary to develop a spiritual growth plan uniquely your own.

Experiencing God Together by David Stoop (Tyndale, 1996).

This book begins with a "Spiritual Inventory" for couples to assess their spiritual life, and continues on to cover topics such as prayer, submission, worship, service, confession, forgiveness, and the need for long-term spiritual exercise. This book will strengthen your marriage by helping you develop spiritual intimacy.

Quiet Times for Couples by H. Norman Wright (Harvest House, 1990).

The 365 daily readings in this best-selling book are beautifully woven around God's Word and are designed to stimulate genuinely open communicaiton between husband and wife. Each day's devotion provides a framework for conversation, making it easier for couples to share about the deeper parts of their lives.

Becoming Soul Mates: Cultivating Spiritual Intimacy in the Early Years of Marriage by Les and Leslie Parrott (Zondervan, 1995).

Every couple has a restless aching, not just to know God individually but to experience God together. But how do you really allow God to fill the soul of your marriage? This book gives you a road map for cultivating rich spiritual intimacy in your relationship. Fifty-two practical weekly devotions help you and your partner cross the hurdles of marriage to grow closer than you've ever imagined. It also contains insights from real-life soul mates like Tony and Peggy Campolo, Bill and Vonette Bright, and dozens of others.

Becoming a Team

The Marriage Builder by Larry Crabb (Zondervan, 1992).

This book cuts to the heart of the biblical view of becoming one flesh in marriage. Crabb argues convincingly that the deepest needs of human personality—security and significance—ultimately cannot be satisfied by a marriage partner. We need to turn to the Lord, rather than our spouse, to satisfy our needs. This frees both partners for "soul oneness," a commitment to minister to our spouses' needs rather than manipulating them to meet our own needs. This book is outstanding, and we recommend it to any couple wanting to build a fulfilling team-based marriage.

He Wins, She Wins: Turn the Battle for Control in Your Marriage Into a "Win-Win" Partnership by Glenn P. Zaepefel (Nelson, 1994).

This book explores a common battle in marriage between the "power partner" and the "passive partner." These styles may be different, and the genders may interchange, but the power games between them are always played the same. If you are feeling the pain of the power-passive struggle in your marriage, this book can help bring your relationship to healing and health. It defines psychological and spiritual hurdles for both partners and offers specific strategies for overcoming this damaging dynamic.

Who's on Top, Who's on Bottom: How Couples Can Learn to Share Power by Robert Schwebel (Newmarket Press, 1994).

This book is built on the premise that, if spouses are to work together as a successful team, they will have to transcend the dominant mode for relationships in our culture: competition. Dr. Schwebel presents the cases of eleven couples. He describes methods for discussing dissatisfaction, expressing resentments, developing calmness, and what to do when cooperation and negotiation fail. This book, however, is not a manual of steps to happiness. It is more about developing an outlook, an attitude, and a vision to guide your marriage.

Finding Help

Marriage Savers: Helping Your Friends and Family Stay Married by Michael J.
   McManus (Zondervan, 1993).

This excellent resource is dedicated to making divorce extinct. The author outlines several strategies anyone can use to help a friend or loved one stay married. Its uniqueness is that it helps those with strong marriages point their friends and relatives with troubled marriages toward resources that will help them stay married. The book is a storehouse of useful information that has been proven to help marriages make it through tough times.

How to Find the Help You Need by Archibald Hart and Timothy Hogan (Zondervan, 1996).

This little book is a gold mine for finding a reputable counselor who can help you in your marriage. The authors know the pitfalls involved in finding qualified help, and they answer common concerns in plain language. They offer insights into saving time and money in counseling, red flags to watch for in a counselor, the kinds of help available, and so on. *How to Find the Help You Need* will point you to the right path for hope, healing, and growth.

MARRIAGE MENTOR MEETING REPORT

Meeting No. _____	Date _____
Your Names: _____	Phone: _____
Mentor Couple: _____	

Thanks for taking the time to fill this out.

The setting for our contact was:

In general, how is your couple doing?

Lousy   *Excellent*

1   2   3   4   5   6   7

Couple's Tough Spots:

Success Stories:

What would help you in the mentoring process?

When is your next scheduled meeting?

MARRIAGE MENTOR
MEETING REPORT

Meeting No. _____ Date _____

Your Names: _____ Phone: _____

Mentor Couple: _____

Thanks for taking the time to fill this out.

The setting for our contact was:

In general, how is your couple doing?

Lousy   *Excellent*

1   2   3   4   5   6   7

© Les and Leslie Parrott

Couple's Tough Spots:

Success Stories:

What would help you in the mentoring process?

When is your next scheduled meeting?

© Les and Leslie Parrott

MARRIAGE MENTOR MEETING REPORT

Meeting No. _____ Date _____

Your Names: _____ Phone: _____

Mentor Couple: _____

Thanks for taking the time to fill this out.

The setting for our contact was:

In general, how is your couple doing?

Lousy   *Excellent*

1   2   3   4   5   6   7

Couple's Tough Spots:

Success Stories:

What would help you in the mentoring process?

When is your next scheduled meeting?

MARRIAGE MENTOR MEETING REPORT

Meeting No. _____	Date _____	
Your Names: _____	Phone: _____	
Mentor Couple: _____		

Thanks for taking the time to fill this out.

The setting for our contact was:

In general, how is your couple doing?

Lousy						*Excellent*
1	2	3	4	5	6	7

Couple's Tough Spots:

Success Stories:

What would help you in the mentoring process?

When is your next scheduled meeting?

MARRIAGE MENTOR
MEETING REPORT

Meeting No. _____ Date _____

Your Names: _____ Phone: _____

Mentor Couple: _____

Thanks for taking the time to fill this out.

The setting for our contact was:

In general, how is your couple doing?

Lousy   *Excellent*

1   2   3   4   5   6   7

Couple's Tough Spots:

Success Stories:

What would help you in the mentoring process?

When is your next scheduled meeting?

© Les and Leslie Parrott

MARRIAGE MENTOR FINAL FEEDBACK FORM

Please complete this evaluation form shortly after you have completed the mentoring program. Please be frank in answering the questions and feel free to use additional pages.

Mentor Couple: _____ Date: _____

Couple we mentored: _____

How would you rate your personal experience as mentors?

Male

Not so hot   *Truly enjoyed it!*

1   2   3   4   5   6   7

Female

Not so hot   *Truly enjoyed it!*

1   2   3   4   5   6   7

How would you rate the effectiveness of the mentoring program as a whole?

Lousy   *Excellent*

1   2   3   4   5   6   7

What was the toughest part of mentoring your couple?

Final Feedback Form, cont.

What could be done to make mentoring a better experience for you?

What could be done to make it a better experience for the couple you mentored?

What advice would you give to another marriage mentor couple?

Do you think you will stay in touch with your mentor couple?

Would you consider mentoring another couple in the future?

Questions Couples Ask

Answers to the Top 100 Marital Questions

Ask yourself the following…

- How can I be honest without hurting my partner's feelings?
- What do we do when one of us is a spender and one of us is a hoarder?
- What can we do to protect our marriage against extramarital affairs?
- How can we be more spiritually intimate as a married couple?

From communication, conflict, and careers to sex, in-laws, and money, *Questions Couples Ask* is your first stop for help with the foremost hurdles of marriage. Drs. Les and Leslie Parrott share cutting-edge insights for the 100 top questions married couples ask. Whether you want to improve your own marriage or nurture the marriages of others, Christianity's premier husband-wife marriage counseling team equips you with expert advice for building a thriving relationship.

Today's married couples find it hard to get the answers they need to their marital questions. They're often so overwhelmed that they don't even know what questions to ask. Les and Leslie Parrott give us the right questions to be thinking about—and the right answers.

Dr. Robert G. Barnes,
Sheridan House Family Ministries

To find answers to these and many other marital questions, pick up your copy of *Questions Couples Ask* at Christian bookstores near you.

Questions Couples Ask
Softcover: 0-310-20754-1

ZondervanPublishingHouse
Grand Rapids, Michigan

A Division of HarperCollinsPublishers

Exciting Marriage Preparation for Today's Young Couples

Saving Your Marriage Before It Starts

Seven Questions to Ask Before (And After) You Marry

Drs. Les & Leslie Parrott

Did you know many couples spend more time preparing for their wedding than they do for their marriage?

Having tasted firsthand the difficulties of "wedding bell blues," Drs. Les and Leslie Parrott show young couples the skills they need to make the transition from "single" to "married" smooth and enjoyable.

Saving Your Marriage Before It Starts is more than a book—it's practically a premarital counseling session. A few questions that will be explored are:

- Have You Faced the Myths of Marriage with Honesty?
- Have You Developed the Habit of Happiness?
- Do You Know How to Fight a Good Fight?

Questions at the end of every chapter help you explore each topic personally. Companion men's and women's workbooks full of self-tests and exercises will help you apply what you learn. And the *Saving Your Marriage Before it Starts* video curriculum will help you to learn and grow with other couples who are dealing with the same struggles and questions.

Here's what the experts are saying about *Saving Your Marriage Before It Starts.*

The Parrotts have a unique way of capturing fresh insights from research and then showing the practical implications from personal experience. This is one of the few 'must read' books on marriage.

Dr. David Stoop
Clinical Psychologist, Co-host of the Minirth Meier New Life Clinics Radio Program

WINNER OF THE 1996 ECPA GOLD MEDALLION BOOK AWARD

Saving Your Marriage Before It Starts **Hardcover:** 0310-49240-8
Saving Your Marriage Before It Starts **Audio Pages:** 0310-49248-3
Saving Your Marriage Before It Starts **Video Curriculum:** 0310-20451-8
Saving Your Marriage Before It Starts **Workbook for Men:** 0310-48731-5
Saving Your Marriage Before It Starts **Workbook for Women:** 0310-48741-2

ZondervanPublishingHouse
Grand Rapids, Michigan

A Division of HarperCollinsPublishers